SURVIVING UNFAMILIAR TERRITORY

First Published in 2021

Beyond The Vale Publishing

Lebogang Tleane

SURVIVING UNFAMILIAR TERRITORY

This book wouldn't have materialized had it not been for my dear mother Nkele Dikomang, who instilled in all her children and grandchildren the love for reading. Your earnest prayers have kept me going more so when I wanted to quit.

To my husband, Sello Tleane, you remain my number one supporter, a true partner from above. Thank you for believing in me, more than I do myself. You are the most patient and considerate person I know.

To my siblings, my womb dividers, Shirley and Pako thanks for always hyping me, for boosting my confidence.

Last but definitely not least, my babies, Roro and Rami. The ones I live for, thank you for being my inspiration.

SURVIVING UNFAMILIAR TERRITORY

A lot of people are afraid of change, more so when they don't know what lies on the other side of their comfort zone. Fear of the unknown is a real thing. Because of this fear, some have sadly missed out on the great opportunity of exploring new things that could change their lives for the better. Take for example a person living in a foreign country, the bold step that they took can help broaden their horizon in the most amazing ways. A person who is taking up a new profession in a totally different field has the chance of learning new things as well as expanding their network. Moving to a new neighbourhood grants one the privilege of making new friends as well as experiencing the thrill of a different setting.

Whatever life-changing decision you make, you are bound to experience different things from what you have been used to. This includes learning a whole lot of new practices as well as unlearning what you have been holding dear. Although life is full of uncertainties, there's nothing as exciting as taking the bold step to experience how people on the other side do things. Embracing change also gives you the chance to find yourself, and learn to be more self-reliant. All of these life-changing experiences won't come to you unless you take that leap of faith and step away from your comfort zone.

Having noted that though, change is not always the best option for everyone. Some people have come to realize that no matter how you consistently water the grass, it's not always greener on the other side. After evaluating your situation, you might find that you are way better off where you are. Life can still be great being surrounded by familiar people and doing activities that you are used to. Besides that, there are a lot of people who have saved themselves hurtful drama, disappointments, loss, financial crisis and all sorts of ugly things by staying put. In most cases, you thrive better when you are in familiar territory. Because of the support of loves ones around, you are able to achieve your dreams and live quite a fulfilling life. Much like plants, some only grow and flourish in an environment they can adapt to.

Sometimes though, moving is not a matter of choice. Life can become so unpredictable and throw you in situations that are way beyond your control. Many people out there are in foreign countries because they had no choice. Some had to flee wars and famine, some are looking for better work opportunities, some have moved to pursue advanced education, whereas others have moved to be with their families who have relocated abroad. Some people got married to foreign nationals among other pressing reasons.

As situations are different, sometimes change is not only about moving to a different country. You can move to a different town because of work or school transfers. Buying or renting a house in a new neighbourhood can be another reason for you to relocate. Hence, we should always have an open mindset that we could move to a different place at any time due to a number of circumstances.

Whatever your reasons for moving to another place, it is up to you to make your stay worthwhile. It is not always easy to adapt to change, but you have to make do in order to survive all the uncertainties life throws at you. Also, note that change doesn't only come with moving physically. There could be some major life-changing shifts you have made in your life. You might have at some point changed sporting clubs, your circle of friends, how you approach life, your diet, or anything that involves getting used to a different setup. Use those kinds of experiences to adapt to major changes you might make in future.

A Border Away

On a daily basis, there is a movement of people from one country to the other. In most cases, people who travel to other countries do so for leisure. Some globe trotters actually save money specifically to cover their travel expenses. We can't blame them, because nothing beats the joy of going on vacation to a different country or exploring a new place. You get to see with your own eyes, the beautiful places that you have probably only heard of or read about. Whether you travel with your family, social club members, friends or colleagues, a getaway for a few days will definitely help to strengthen the bond you have through the quality time spent together. Time off from home also grants you the opportunity to somewhat escape your reality, to refresh, recharge as well as unwind.

Some people, on the other hand, do not travel only for a short period of time. They have moved to another country to make it their permanent place of residence. A person who has moved kilometres away from home fleeing war and famine definitely isn't doing that for pleasure. Life sadly happened! Many people have to further their studies abroad because the level of education in their county is not that advanced. Others have moved to au pair, to take gap years, to seek better medical attention, or moved to join their spouses abroad. It does not matter what circumstances have caused you to move, leaving your home to stay in a different country is an experience easier said than done.

The moment you decide to move, there is no doubt that you will get overwhelmed with a lot of mixed feelings. One thing that will constantly ring in your head is the new life that lies ahead. You wonder how locals are going to receive you, the new challenges that might come along the way, the opportunities that will present themselves, the new things you are going to learn, and the old habits you might have to do away with. Moving to a new country also comes with that zest of starting life afresh in a place where you have no history or reputation. No one is going to judge you based on their experiences with you. Every time you think about this life, you can't help but get excited and nervous all at the same time.

Although grass has proven to be greener on the other side for a lot of people, the mere fact that you are moving away from your comfort zone is a challenge in itself. Just imagine having to move to a place where the weather is completely different from home, where the food eaten is a whole new experience, where the language barrier makes communication almost impossible, where the culture is something of a shock, among other things. Thinking about all this can make you even more uneasy about moving. Granted, the difficulties will always be there, but it is up to you to make yourself as comfortable as possible in your new home. Embrace the changes and accept things the way they are for you to survive.

Moving also requires a whole lot of admin. You have to do research prior to moving, arrange and coordinate the trip. In some cases, as the traveller, you have to make your own accommodation arrangements. Even just moving across the street, is a lot of work. It is up to you to make sure that everything you need is packed, and that the place you are moving to, is in a good state. How much more so, when moving to a different country! It will surely require extra effort on your part.

One can travel to the best places in the world, but nothing beats the comfort and love of where you come from. Home is without a doubt where the heart is. The comfort of it all enables you the opportunity to flourish in all kinds of ways. But if you are permanently moving to a new place, you had better make it feel homely so that you can enjoy your stay.

Prepare For a Different Life

It goes without saying that life is going to be different, so be prepared for the changes. Preparations can never be enough though since this is not just a holiday for a short period of time. You are literally moving to this place to make it your home. Be ready for the challenges that will come along the way. As you prepare for the big move, brace yourself that in so many ways, life is going to be different from the one that you have been living. This is the time for you to prove to yourself and others that you are a global citizen who can easily adapt to life in a different environment.

Prior to moving, do thorough research about your host country. Being aware of what lies ahead will minimize your anxiety as well as help you adjust quickly by the time you reach your destination. The research will also make you more confident about your move since now you have an idea about this new place. By discovering a lot of facts about your new home, you'll find more reasons to fall in love with it and stand by your decision no matter who says what. The internet has made it easier for travellers to familiarize themselves with the places they want to visit, so make use of it. Check out how the weather is, the culture, language and so forth. Most importantly, as an outsider, it is imperative to know how foreign nationals are treated in that particular county. If it is a country of a different race from you, find out if the locals are racists or accommodating before you move. Thus, you will avoid putting yourself in danger of becoming a victim of racial violence or a xenophobic attack.

Another thing, since you are a foreign national, this means you will be away from your family and friends, and will probably be lonely in your first few months or even years. Now you have to prepare for life without most of your loved ones around you. There might be no one physically present to encourage you to celebrate your wins, or guide you when you need to be shown the way. If you have always relied on others to help or hype you, this is the time to learn to be self-reliant. Prepare yourself for a life where your accomplishments might not be celebrated to the fullest. A life where you might not get recognized. There will be situations where your achievements might rub some people off the wrong way. If you come across such, modesty is going to be the quality to live by, to avoid unnecessary squabbles.

One justice you can do yourself is to visit your host country prior to moving, if possible. It beats doing research online or getting information from elsewhere. Going there in advance will help you to understand how life is like in that particular country. This will also help you avoid stress when it comes to covering certain logistics. You can use your trip to visit immigration offices to find out what is really expected of you as a foreign national. You can also check out your embassy in that county to know the steps to take should you find yourself in a desperate situation. You can also visit a few local neighbourhoods to see which areas are the safest, the ones which are most welcoming and would be best for you and your family. You may even be able to find a place to stay, by contacting some real estate agents in advance or arranging viewings with individual landlords or roommates.

Another thing, before moving, it is also important that you sort out the relevant paperwork. Go and do the correct Visa as soon as possible. Also, make sure that your travelling documents are up to date. When it comes to managing your expenses, find out how much locals are paying for things like utilities, transport, basic needs and so forth. By so doing, you won't make unnecessary financial blunders when you are far away from home. You can never make enough preparation, but one thing is for sure, the little that you do will help to make your stay smoother.

Make It Feel Like Home

Getting to explore a new place, is one of the most exciting things about moving, at least for some people. The whole adventure of checking out places is always something to look forward to every day. In your first few months or even years in your host country, you will practically become a glorified tourist. If this is your first time there, most of the things that locals and other people consider ordinary will be fascinating to you. When others have had it about a particular thing or place, you on the other hand find it mind-blowing. You can't help but gush over everything you come across.

Every single day, you want to go out and sightsee more new places. Malls, restaurants and monuments, are there to give you the much needed fresh experience. Most places you visit will make you feel like a kid in a candy store, simply because they are to die for. The mere fact that you will not know a lot of people, exploring will keep you occupied and less lonely. You will be kept busy by taking pictures of everything you set your eyes on and share on your social media platforms. Every time you call home, all you talk about is what you get to see on a daily basis.

Well, everything has limits, and so is exploring. As time goes by, it definitely will not be as exciting as it was at the start. You cannot live all of your life going out and about. At some point, you need to settle down and mature. That is when reality sinks in, and you start to miss something familiar. You start to notice that the place you have moved to is not all that great. As you get over the first excitement, you might even notice personality traits you did not anticipate from others. Same as visiting friends or family; all you can think of is for the visit to end when you are not enjoying your stay. Sadly moving abroad doesn't afford you the privilege to just up and leave. This is now your home, the sooner you make it work, the better.

Now, this is the time for you to draw inspiration from people who have stayed for years in foreign countries. Undoubtedly, where you come from, there are foreign nationals around, and a lot of them have thrived, even much better than locals. This is because, instead of feeling sorry for themselves, they made the most of the situation. Take this opportunity to advance yourself. Taking time to learn how things are done, might also make you bond more with the locals. This will help you to make friends quickly and fill that loneliness gap. It is all up to you to make the place as comfortable as if you are back home.

Embracing your new home does not mean that you have to constantly bash where you come from. Yes, you will have an audience willing to listen, but this can really burn you bad in future. Xenophobic attacks normally happen to foreign nationals whose situation at home is unfavourable. Some locals feel that a lot of foreign nationals are there to take opportunities reserved for them. Saying negative things about your home might make this statement seem true. Some people will question your motive of moving from your home, all the more risking being treated as a lesser human being, who is there out of desperation.

Blending in also doesn't mean losing your identity as a person. Remember that you are an ambassador of your place of origin. Not a lot of people are knowledgeable about other countries, yours included. Take this golden opportunity to tell the locals about where you come from. Your home country might not be as advanced as your host country, but the truth is, it has shaped who you are. Your history makes such a big part of you, so don't be ashamed to share that aspect of your life with anyone showing interest. As much as it is greener pastures that might have influenced your move, always try to speak positively about where you come from. By so doing, you will have a piece of home with you all the time.

Learn to Start From Scratch

When you move to a new place, you try by all means to pack most of the things that you are going to need there. Some people even prefer using prominent moving companies, to make sure all their belongings are safely packed and taken to their new residence. It is a tiring but rewarding task. How so? As you pack your stuff, you will realize that some of your belongings are just clutter that needs to go. There is no greater pleasure than giving away the things that you do not really need to those who will appreciate them. After all, you can always get some new items in the area you are moving to. I mean who would want to go around carrying old things to a new place? This is the time for a fresh start!

Having noted that though, there will always be valuable assets that you worked hard for over the years, but for some reason cannot take along. One such asset is a house. It is probably one of the biggest achievements of your life to have a place you call your own. Sadly this is one asset you cannot move when you relocate. So, either you sell it, rent it out, or leave it under the care of a trusted someone. There are also other assets like cars and some household furniture which are better off left behind when you move. This means that wherever you are going, you will have to more or less start life from the beginning. In these tough financial times, you will be faced with not only having to adapt to life in a new environment but also spending money to buy some necessities.

If you are faced with this kind of situation, do not despair. Starting afresh can be such an exciting experience. You get motivated to get things done all over again. Take comfort in knowing that there are a lot of people out there who lost almost everything they have, but some made major comebacks. Granted, this might be a little tricky because you will be starting all over again, away from home. It is a real challenge, but you can turn it into some kind of an achievable goal. When the odds are against you, this is all the more reason for you to show people what you are made of. It might seem a bit far-fetched, but it is possible for a foreign national to start from scratch and acquire assets they have never even dreamt of having. Try by all means to find your strength in letting go, instead of holding on to superfluous material possessions. Who knows, by letting go of some stuff, you might have your chance to experience even bigger and better things.

The reality of the matter though, when you start from scratch, is that you have to start from somewhere. In this instance, financial literacy is your armour. Before taking that bold step of relocating, make sure that you have a financial plan in place. Important things like your housing costs, living costs, entertainment costs, transport and travel insurance costs should be covered and calculated beforehand. You also have to understand the currency value of the country you are moving to. This will help you make sound financial decisions, and not be scammed easily. You also have to make budgets that you will be able to stick to, because chances are that high no one is going to bail you out when you are high and dry.

Not only are you going to start afresh financially, you are also going to learn how to adjust to the new place. Knowing your way around requires an effort on your part. On top of everything else, you have to make new friends (probably also new enemies, come to think of it!). You might also have to learn the language spoken as well as adapt to a new culture. All of these changes are going to make you feel like you are starting life all over again. It can be daunting at first, but having an open mind will help you cope. Humbling yourself as a beginner, will make starting afresh in this new place a bit easier.

Do Your Best to Make Ends Meet

It does not matter whether you are in your home country, or a foreign national, you need to have a means of survival. In these tough economic times, it is imperative that you earn a living. For those who moved to foreign countries to study or work, money doesn't become much of an issue in most cases. This happens in instances where your organization has transferred you outside the country, when you have been offered a job outside, or when the organization you work for, or government sends you outside to further your studies. There will always be a salary or an allowance to help you make ends meet.

But what now if you are moving out of your country because of pressing matters like looking for a job, searching for better opportunities or fleeing war and famine? When people in such situations relocate, they are hopeful of creating a better life for themselves and their families in a new place. They also want to integrate into a new society where they can better their situations and possibly become citizens in their host countries. Such individuals move, not entirely because they fancy staying in foreign countries, but because the situation at home is tough and desperate. Just like everyone else, they need to eat, to clothe, to have a roof over their head, as well as provide for their families. For all of these basic needs to be met, one has to have a substantial source of income. But because the circumstances you left under are of desperation, you might find yourself destitute without a plan in a foreign place. How can you then make your situation better, if you moved not by choice, but by default?

The reality of the matter is that finding a good job, and moving up the corporate ladder, is going to be extremely difficult. Even if you do manage to find a good job, by virtue of you being a foreigner, you might have to work the hardest, just to get half the recognition the locals at your workplace get. You are most likely to be bullied at work, more so in situations where you advance quickly. At times you might even have to take a job that you never thought you would do because, at the end of the day, you need to have a salary. Although some jobs might not be easy, keep telling yourself that you came there to work, as well as to provide for yourself and your loved ones. The little that you get will sustain you until you get the better job of your dreams. Console yourself with the fact that even some locals are faced with the same situation as you. In these times, it is actually tough for everyone, regardless of citizenship.

Although earning a living is important, avoid being so obsessed with finding work that you end up saying yes to something that'll leave you with scars. Most foreign nationals are ready to take whatever job is available when they first enter their host country. This is not always wise because once certain employers recognize your desperation, they might be tempted to give you the less desirable and dangerous roles in the company. You might have to work longer hours and get paid a meagre salary. This will definitely add to your challenges, making you realize that moving was not the best option for you. Quite often, undocumented immigrants find themselves faced with employment injustices. Even when you are not happy, you cannot air your grievances, making the exploitation escalate. Try by all means to have the correct documentation that allows you to be in that country, as well as work there.

A wise move will be to choose your host country carefully if you are looking for greener pastures. Make sure the place doesn't have a high unemployment rate. The fact of the matter is that some places are much worse than your home country. You might be jumping from the frying pan straight into the fire without even realizing it. If you have come to the conclusion that leaving your home country is your best option, then be prepared to work hard as you make ends meet. Keep looking for better opportunities and never miss one. Everything that helps you earn money, provided it's legal and safe, is worth investigating.

Overcome the Language Barrier

Without a doubt, language is the epitome of communication. To a certain degree, it is imperative that you and the person you are chatting with should have at least one language in common for a smooth conversation. Although English is widely used in many countries around the world, not everyone understands the language. In many places, some people prefer to communicate in what is normally referred to as the 'Mother Tongue'. They take pride and feel they can express themselves perfectly well in a language they grew up exposed to. So, if you move to a place where a language you are not familiar with is spoken, a lot of challenges should be anticipated. You won't be able to express yourself the best way you would have if you use your own language from home. This can sadly force you to not voice your opinions and you resort to keeping quiet instead.

Do not despair though, when faced with such a challenge. There are ways to break this language barrier obstacle. Your best option is to learn the language spoken around the community you have moved to. Although this is your best shot, learning a new language, more so as an adult is not easy. It needs time, dedication, patience and a sharp mind. The good thing is that you do not necessarily have to be fluent. As long as you can get your message across, you are good to go. Have a local friend nearby, who can assist you to learn faster. Many locals will surely appreciate your genuine attempts to communicate in their mother tongue. This will also give you the opportunity to meet more people, as your presence begins to get noticed. Learning a new language can also benefit you in aspects of your professional life.

However, we cannot overlook the fact that speaking the local language can also come with a few challenges for you. Being as fluent as the locals is not always achievable. This can knock down your confidence, more especially when people laugh at your efforts. Again, some locals can make your life a living hell after picking up that you have a different accent to them. Remember, not everyone appreciates having a new person in their territory. This is where the subtle xenophobic attacks come to play. People mimic how you pronounce certain words, while others erupt into fits of laughter once you open your mouth. Any person who goes through all of this will definitely find it a challenge to put their point across, well, unless you are the type that can stand your ground even when outnumbered.

The reality of the matter is that you are not in your own comfort zone, but you need to make it work. How about you take the lemons thrown at you and make some refreshing lemonade? Even the most negative of situations have a positive side to them. The fact that your accent is different makes you stand out. Open minded locals, will want to learn more about you, your culture, your language, and everything else that defines your origins. You will find that there are people who are mesmerized by that beautiful unique accent of yours. They love it when you speak and will encourage you to communicate more. Now those are your people, your new tribe and you should stick to them.

Do not worry yourself about a few haters, not everyone has a problem with someone who doesn't speak the same language as them. Because you are struggling with the language, some people will reach out to you and will be happy to assist you in every possible way. Some people have been blessed with pure hearts that see beyond language. Do not let language become a barrier for you to move to another country, and if you are already abroad, try by all means not to let this challenge steal your joy and make your stay miserable.

Appreciate the Cultural Difference

Culture is such an important aspect of many people's lives. It is one thing that makes a group of people stand out from the rest. You know that a person is from a certain region without them having to mention it, by observing how they conduct themselves. Their dress sense or code, how they speak and their general way of doing things can tell you what part of the world they come from. How are you going to handle yourself then, if the country you are moving to has a totally different culture from where you come from? Are you going to follow suit or just stick to your unique self? Are you going to embrace their culture, or you will keep on pointing out what you don't appreciate about how they do things?

When in Rome, do as the Romans do. This famous saying simply emphasizes the importance of adapting yourself to the customs of the place you are visiting or moving to. As a foreign national, always have the mindset that you are going to experience new and totally different things. This will make it easy for you to quickly adapt when you come across 'shocking' things. If you want to learn quickly, follow the lead of those who know the ropes so that you are able to do things the way they are done. As someone living in a foreign country, do yourself justice to quickly understand and appreciate the culture of the place you are moving to. The quicker you learn how people do things, the better you will adjust. You will also blend in quickly in your new home.

It is not easy though to adjust just like that overnight. If you are not a well-travelled person, you are bound to experience some serious culture shock. We might be all human, but the truth of the matter is that we do things differently according to where we are in the world. In some places, it is a norm for men to wear skirts and head wraps. Whereas in other places it is taboo to see a woman rocking a pair of trousers, drinking alcohol, smoking cigarettes or speaking up for themselves. Some places are way too conservative, while in other places, individuals are given the choice to live their life the way they see fit. A conservative environment might make you feel like a prisoner. On the other hand, if you have a sensitive conscience, you might not enjoy your stay in a country where everybody is too free to do as they please.

The best way to help you cope with a culture you are not used to is to embrace other people's way of doing things, as opposed to always criticizing. When it comes to food, try to eat like a local. There is absolutely no harm in exploring different meals. Try learning how to cook some of the national dishes or find a spot where they specifically sell popular traditional dishes. You can also get yourself some clothes that are normally worn in the area that you have moved to. Find out which clothes can be worn by everyone, and for what occasion before your ignorance offends other people. Watching the local TV content, as well as listening to local radio programs will help you get used to how the locals live their lives.

As discussed in the past chapter, research will come in handy. The internet and books provide information about every place you can think of around the world. Use it to find out the traditions as well as customs of the new place you are about to move to. Research your host country to find out what life is like for locals and how tourists and foreigners fit into the puzzle. Find out what is socially acceptable and what is taboo to avoid offending other people. The trick is to behave as you would do in a new workplace. Ask those who have been there for ages if there's anything specific you should do to fit in your new home. Also, hold back when it comes to promoting your own interest, rather watch and learn. When you are informed of the expectations required from you, it will be easier for you to embrace the culture.

Build Solid Relationships

One way to enjoy life to the fullest is to have great relationships with people around you. A healthy relationship with other people is vital for our mental as well as emotional wellbeing. We practically thrive better if we are on good terms with others. During our happy times, we are able to share our joy with our loved ones, and when we are down there is always someone ready to listen and pick us up. Moreover, we also need people with who we can hang around, have meaningful conversations with and just do this life thing with. That is why it is vital in life to build strong, healthy and loving relationships.

This is no exception when you have moved to a different country. You obviously are leaving your friends, family (in some cases), colleagues and neighbours behind. This doesn't mean that now you have to be a loner, who spends most of their time watching TV, reading or doing absolutely nothing. Wherever you go, you still have to make good relationships with others. Since you have moved to a new country, you are going to need to be on good terms with most people you come across. Be it in your neighbourhood, at work, at school or wherever you spend most of your time, a good reputation is very important. Beautiful friendships and positive relationships will make your stay even more enjoyable.

Having noted that though, it is not going to be an easy walk around the park for you to make friends with people you just met, especially those from a different culture as yours. Obviously, when you get to a new place you find people who are already in friendships, which go back a long way. They are best friends with people they have known for most of their lives. You, on the other hand, are just a newbie who has just arrived. It is quite common with many people to trust one of their own, rather than a person they have just come across. You still need to work hard to gain the local's trust and acceptance before you become part of their friendship circles. It can take time for them to warm up to you for various reasons.

Sometimes because you excel in certain areas, you can appear intimidating to some locals, and they will resort to distancing themselves from you as a way to 'humble' you. Some might just interpret your excellence as arrogance. In some instances, foreign nationals are not being treated right because some locals are under the impression that they are going to 'steal' opportunities from them. Well, we can't argue the fact that a lot of people have fled their countries for a better life. But there are many cases where foreigners come to certain countries to offer scarce skill services. If this is the case with you, try to humble yourself so that no local feels threatened by you. Do not at any point make them conclude that you think you are better than them (even if you are). Let the locals take the lead in most things, just to make them feel that they have an upper hand in their environment.

As difficult as it seems, forming great relationships and bonds in a new place is possible. A lot of people have made great friends, and even families in the countries they now reside in. You too can have that with a number of locals you come across. Work hard to break any stereotype associated with the place you come from so that people can be interested in having a relationship with you. With caution, put yourself out there, and reach out to people who your soul vibes with. You can join social clubs, go out with your colleagues and introduce yourself to a few neighbours without appearing to be too much. Also take advantage of social media platforms, who knows, you might come across groups of people from your country around your hood. You could also search for your fellow countrymen online so that you can form relationships with those to who you relate to.

Fit In Smoothly

Any new person in an area is bound to stand out. Their sense of style, how they speak, sometimes skin tone, are some of the things that will make locals realize that a person is not one of their own. In some cases, it's all nice and cool to stand out and feel like some sort of a celebrity with all the attention you will be getting. A lot of people will definitely find you interesting, simply because you are different from the rest. People who stand out from the crowd are noticeable and always make solid lasting impressions. A person who stands out also shows that they live a life true to themselves and have no pressure to live a life that others expect of them.

Standing out is not always the best way to live though. Unfortunately when you have moved to a new country, by default you are going to stand out. As much as you would love to blend in with the rest of the people around you quickly, standing out might be your reality for some time. Depending on the place where you are from, most things about you can bring too much attention your way. If this isn't how you roll, the whole experience can be daunting. We are all different, and some people do not fancy being the centre of attraction. Maybe you are one of those individuals, and you prefer fewer eyes on you. Also being identified as an outsider is not really cool. You just want to be treated like everyone else.

Even if you have moved to a country that you really like, it might happen that you do not get the reception you anticipated. You can become an outcast for a long time and be made to feel unwelcome. Some locals can make your experience so hard that you will wish to go back home in a heartbeat. As sad as the situation is, try to not make hasty decisions and take it one day at a time. Honestly, it is not always going to be easy to fit in, the moment you arrive. It will take time for you to adjust, and also for some people to warm up to you. It is going to take time for you to learn the language as well as change your dress sense if needs be. Also bear in mind that certain locals do not fancy having an outsider on their turf. They only want those from their tribe or area around them. Fitting in will thus become almost impossible.

Instead of feeling miserable from all the negativity, take this opportunity to learn more about the people in this area. Past issues like apartheid, racism and some traditions might be the reason they are not so accommodating. Your empathy will help you not step on anyone's toes, to not rush things, and this might move locals to tolerate you better. Go the extra mile to try and make friends with those who look beyond nationality. Getting out there and interacting with people with similar interests as you, is a great way to make yourself (and others) realize that we are all the same beyond nationality. You also have to be content with the fact that, you would not fit in everywhere and with just anyone. You are better off without following certain trends, and hanging out with people who do not share the same values as you.

Now that you are in a new place, you are faced with a multitude of challenges, homesickness being one of them. When some locals isolate you, it makes the whole situation even worse. Something that can help you cope with all the loneliness is to stay in touch with people from back home. Use the time you are cast aside to call home, write them letters, and even get them special gifts. At the end of the day, your friends and family are the ones who know how to cheer you up during dark days.

Another thing that can help you, is to continue doing things that you used to enjoy while back home. This will surely help you to see that at times fitting in can be a little overrated. In the meantime, use grace to grow into this new place. You need to remember why you relocated, and that should also give you the motivation to try a little harder to settle in.

Find Ways to Beat the Loneliness

It is normal to feel lonely when you are away from home for some time. How much more now, that you are permanently based in a foreign country? As a person considering relocating, prepare yourself for days, weeks, months or even years of loneliness. There will be times when you badly miss home, your family, your friends, and just how you used to do things while you were back home. Even if you are in great company, when that feeling comes, you will still feel so lonely.

Another thing that can bring about loneliness is when you fail to click with those around you. You come to realize that no matter how hard you try, connecting with the locals you meet proves to be too difficult a mission. This might be because you do not share the same interests as the people you come across. In some instances, it might be due to the fact that those you meet simply do not like you as a person. Yes, you will have to make peace with the reality that there are people who prefer not to associate themselves with foreign nationals. It is common for some individuals to have a stereotypical mindset when it comes to outsiders. As sad as it is, it happens and you have to prepare for that kind of reception. All of these factors and more will undoubtedly make trying to form strong bonds with locals seem impossible. Of course, this could be something you might have expected prior to moving, but still, being cast aside is going to make you feel so unwanted and definitely lonely.

Before you start getting miserable about what is happening to you, try to figure out if this 'isolation' is just an imaginary feeling in your head. At times, we create a picture in our minds that ends up looking like a reality. Just because you are not invited to certain activities, gatherings or parties you might arrive at the conclusion that your nationality has something to do with it. Seeing a group of locals doing a particular activity together might leave you feeling unwanted. Another thing, being around people who speak a language that you don't understand, or have conversations about experiences you were not part of, can make you feel like an outcast. Because you cannot relate to a lot of things, you are bound to feel lonely, or worse feel useless, making your stay unbearable. By virtue of you, convinced that you are always left out, every little plan made without your consultation will trigger you.

Yes, sometimes it will happen that you are being isolated deliberately. Some people won't want you around. Instead of feeling down, approach the situation with a positive mindset. You won't always have a hundred per cent control over how people feel about you, but you can control how that affects your life. It is not nice to feel lonely and left out, but rest assured that things can turn around for the better. Although you are far away from home, there are lots of things you can do to cheer yourself up.

Instead of looking at the negative occurrences, observe things that bring you joy and make you feel fulfilled. Pursue those things at a wider spectrum. If you are into music, try to explore it even more. You can collect old and new music, learn how to play a particular instrument or compose your own songs. If you are into working out, download as many workout videos as possible. Or better yet, join a gym nearby so you can mingle with those who have the same passion as you. If you are passionate about a particular sport, why not identify a local team that you can rally behind? You can always try volunteering for something that is close to your heart and through this, you will keep yourself busy as well as meet new people, who will ignite your soul.

Embrace Being Alone

Just like the previous chapter emphasized, relocating to a different place where no one knows you, is going to make you feel more alone than you were back home. As time goes by, the thrill of a new place is going to wear off and loneliness will kick in. You will find yourself missing even the simplest things like your traditional food, television programmes, communicating in your mother tongue and everything you used to take for granted. Thinking about all this might make one sceptical about relocating.

Come to think of it though, being alone is not as bad as it sounds. Of course, the thought that comes to mind when you think about it, is that you are going to be miserable and feel left out of a lot of things. You also think of the boredom that lies ahead among other things. Do yourself justice and change those thoughts for a moment and look at the brighter side. Being alone is definitely a golden opportunity for you to enjoy your own company, which is the best thing you can do for yourself. You won't have to rely on the next person for happiness or fulfilment. Being surrounded by people all the time is not always the best way to live. As much as it feels good to be in the company of others, nothing beats taking time out to focus on yourself. Being by yourself takes away all the negative vibes of gossiping, trolling, being put down by certain individuals and so forth.

Embracing being alone is not easy though. Once you feel a bit lonely, it can be really easy to wallow in it. You start to feel unloved and envy those who have great company around them. The worst thing that you can do when feeling like this, is putting on sad songs and thinking of the life you once had. Instead, spin your situation around and do all the things you can enjoy doing solo. Obviously, you can't have everything in common with the people you hang with, now this is the time to do those activities that set you apart. Whether it's checking out museums, working out, watching movies or going to the park, when you do activities that bring you joy, you will without a doubt appreciate your being alone.

Before jumping headfirst into having as many friends as you can get, this is the time for you to enjoy your new-found independence. As a loner, there is no one pressurizing you to follow trends that don't even like to begin with. You no longer have the pressure of doing things just to please a crowd, who do not necessarily have your best interest at heart. This is your chance to go out there and do what you want without feeling awkward from all the judgment. Try out new things and take worthy risks if you should. You didn't relocate to be all bored and miserable. You have no one to please but yourself, so go out there and do you.

This is also the opportunity for you to upgrade yourself. Now that you have free time, why not use it to advance your studies? If you relocated because of work, then find a short course that you can pursue when you knock off or during your off days. You can also do side hustles like nail art, photography, baking, offering babysitting services, or anything that you are passionate about. If you moved to a new country to further your studies, you can look for a part-time job in your spare time. A lot of students work as waiters, bartenders, and do other odd jobs just to have extra cash and kill time. You can also learn a new skill, while at it. There are so many interesting things to learn like playing certain musical instruments, painting, fashion design and so forth. If you look at it from the right angle, being alone can do you so much good.

Home-Sickness Has a Cure

Home is definitely where the heart is. It doesn't matter the circumstances you left your country under, at some point you are going to miss home. Even if you are having the most fun and life is good where you are currently based, home will always be the epitome of fulfilment. Hence there will be moments when you really feel like packing your belongings and going back to where you came from. You will find yourself yearning for that familiar environment, where you could hang around those you grew up with, as well as do activities that you used to enjoy back in the day.

It doesn't matter that you have family or friends around you, there are going to be those moments when you miss physically being home. There are no two ways about it. When that feeling comes, it doesn't mean you have hate towards your host country. It also doesn't mean that you appreciate your host country or those around you any less. It is perfectly normal for one to feel this way after some time away from home. It is just that at that moment, you wish you were somewhere else, with a different crowd appreciating a familiar place. How then are you going to make yourself feel better when you miss home?

43

Before such feelings knock at your doorstep, make a habit of talking to your friends and family back home regularly. Consistently communicating with loved ones from home is a way to prevent feeling all alone. The fact that you have those you love at speed dial, makes you feel like you always have a bit of home with you. You constantly share sound conversations about the things you relate to. Those who have cut off close ones from home when life got better are at a higher risk of feeling miserable when homesick. Do yourself justice, and try as much as you can to avoid the mistake of neglecting loved ones from home. As much as life has changed for the better, there is certainly a place where you started from, and that's home. Just because you have moved to a new place, probably with better opportunities, never ever shun or belittle those who are back home. Otherwise, when you really get homesick, you will have no one to make you feel a little better.

One thing that can help you avoid constantly getting homesick, is to accept and face your current reality. Keep on reminding yourself fact that you have moved to a new place to start a new life. The sooner you become content with the fact that your loved ones are far, the better you will cope. It doesn't mean that you are completely doing away with anything to do with your past, you are simply appreciating life with new people in a different place. Always looking back will not help you, instead, you will miss home so badly that you won't enjoy your stay. You will also loathe your host country and everyone around you. Yes, home will always be in your heart, but also give yourself a chance to make your host country as comfortable as if you were born there. This is the time for you to out and talk to people here in your new home. It is the time to make new friends, go hang out with some people to get that feel of the new.

To fill that gap of not being physically home, you can bring an element of home to you. Listen to your traditional music, watch shows from home on YouTube and cook your favourite staple food among other things. Another thing that can help is spending time with other foreign nationals. Even if they do not come from the same country as you, they are definitely in the same boat as you. Picking their minds on how they deal with this kind of situation will help you. It is entirely up to you to make your situation better.

Graciously Handle Negativity

Everyone wants to be loved, in fact, all of us deserve to be loved by those around us. Sadly, life doesn't guarantee us that we will always receive the same energy we give out. You can be the best person ever but still rub others the wrong way. A person who is always determined to find your short comings will never appreciate any good deed from you. Another thing, we exist among people who are going through their own problems, and they sadly bleed on us. So, whether you are a local or a foreign national, always know that no matter what kind of person you are, not everyone will fall for you.

The situation can be quite unbearable if you are a foreigner who is disliked by some locals. Imagine being subjected to ridicule and treated worse than other people simply because you are from outside the country. You will feel like that adopted child who is least loved by their foster parents. For the lack of use of a better word, it sucks! There will be those people ready to take you down, dying to tell you off as well as put you in your place. It gets quite hectic if this behaviour is repeated over and over again. This can occur at work, at school, in the neighbourhood, at social clubs or from those you consider as friends.

As mentioned at the beginning of the chapter, we all want to be loved, for us to be the best we can be. But when we are treated badly, this can trigger feelings of anger, loneliness, hurt, and confusion. When we are always put down, we tend to question our self-worth and can spiral into depression. If this kind of treatment goes as far as social media bullying, you can go to the extent of shying away from sharing posts, blocking some individuals or exiting certain platforms altogether.

Dealing with hate, more especially subtle xenophobia, can be tricky. You can't do much about being hated for your nationality. If a person is going to mock you based on that, no matter how brutal they become, this is not a battle worth engaging in. Try by all means to ignore it. Remember that you are outnumbered, and always getting involved in unnecessary conflicts can do you more harm than good. Learn to let certain things slide, and not sweat the small stuff. Although some people will make it their mission to make your life a living hell, note that not all locals are like that. Not everyone is going to hate you for absolutely no reason, some people have lives. There will be those who will love you still, and no matter how few they are, appreciate them and ignore the ones harbouring bitter feelings.

If the hate happens online, the block button is your best option. Blocking a person doesn't necessarily mean you hate them, it is simply done because you want to be at peace even when you are on social media. Sad people are always finding ways to bring others down in the form of jokes, do your best to not fall into their trap. Block and mute to protect your inner peace. After getting bullies off your space, you will be free to post whatever content you want to share without expecting vile negativity from the comments section. Remain only with friends and followers who are not about cyberbullying.

Another way to deal with haters is to show them love and empathy. Sometimes all the hate that you are receiving has nothing to do with you, but everything to do with the perpetrator's past and current struggles. Some people will be going through their own drama, and they lash out at the nearest victim. Their opinions are all about what is going on in their miserable lives and they are using you to make themselves feel better. At times being kind to them despite how they treat you can go a long way. Have them over at your home for lunches, compliment them and always be there when they need help. There is already so much hate in the world, so do your best to spread love when you can.

Bring Something to the Table

A lot of the time when a person is invited to a dinner party, a wedding or any celebration, they bring a small gift. This is not a form of payment, but it is a way to show courtesy and appreciation for the invitation. If you don't know the host that well, bringing a gift can also help to strengthen your bond, and more invitations will roll in future. Surely as a foreigner, you are not going to give anyone you come across gifts in order to have a great relationship with them. But still, you need to bring something to the table. How so?

Say for example you are moving to join a spouse who is a local in your host country. You are going to become part of a new family, which has a different culture from yours. This is without a doubt going to prove to be a challenge for you. Along the way, you are going to step on other family members' toes, and sadly in some instances, you might not be treated right. And, as a foreign in-law, you might have to work extra hard to prove that you are not a kind of a mail-order spouse. You would not want to appear as if the marriage was your ticket to a good life, or it was your way out of a certain situation. As much as jobs are scarce, work hard to have a source of income. By doing so, you will minimize the chances of you becoming a subject of ridicule when prejudice issues come up, and yes, they will!

Even if you relocate to look for a better opportunity, make sure you come through for locals when things work out for you. If your business venture bears fruits, give locals a chance by employing them. Often foreigners will rather have people from their home country work for them as opposed to locals. Well, some may reason that it is easier to work with those whose background you understand better. Others might say, they opt to give the disadvantaged a chance. All of these reasons are valid but remember locals are also looking for employment. You also do not want to rub up citizens as well as officials, the wrong way. As much as you relocated there because things were not working out at home, now that you are starting to do well, it is only fair to show appreciation to your host country.

In some countries, immigrants have introduced new products, fresh business activities, employment opportunities and some have brought scarce skills. If you have come to offer scarce skills, or are coming with employment opportunities, do not look down on the locals, more so those who are struggling to make ends meet. A lot of the times locals suffer at the hands of foreign nationals who have employed them. Among other things, they give local workers a meagre salary, treat them badly, expose them to unfavourable working conditions and so forth. This affects the relationship between foreigners and locals in general. Those who have been treated unfairly eventually take out their pain and frustrations on innocent people who have nothing to do with their experiences. So instead of contributing to the division among nationalities, come with peace, tranquillity and grace.

Another vital contribution from foreign nationals is that they bring more diversity into their host nation and create a diverse world as well. Your presence in the country that is hosting you, plays a major role in creating a global community. Even if you do not bring anything tangible to benefit others, never ever doubt the impact that you have as a foreign national in your host country.

Know When to Dim Your Light and When to Shine

When we accomplish a certain goal or achieve something, it is only normal that we would want others to celebrate with us. Social media is one of the main mediums that a lot of people use to share their joy. Sadly sometimes we might need to hold on for a minute from posting and sharing just to avoid stepping on other people's toes. Nothing is as frustrating as having to dim your light to accommodate the feelings of others, but such is life. We live in a world where we have to put others first for our own sanity.

Normally, people who are out there about their capabilities and achievements are regarded as arrogant. Such individuals also risk being targets from criminals as well as people who want to put them in their place. In order to avoid frictions, some people avoid becoming too much for others, too smart, too wise, too happy, or too beautiful. They keep quiet about what they have, or how far they have come against all odds. Even if you have nothing, once some people realize that you have the potential to become something, jealousy can creep in and they will use every kind of loophole to always put you down.

As a foreign national coming from a developing country, some locals will automatically want you to be beneath them. Because it is their backyard, locals would want to be ahead in literally everything. Be it opinions, privilege or material gains, they always aim for position one. In some instances, you might be in situations where you have to hide your material possessions, your strong views, opinions, desires, and boundaries from others. As sad as it is, it makes you less of a target every time they feel like venting about foreign nationals. At times you might even be forced to keep your pain to yourself. This is because some people can go to the extent of dismissing your true feelings as something not that deep.

Once they sense some potential in you, some locals won't let you slide on anything. There will be some gaslighting, being cast aside, malicious gossip, being told off, and verbal attacks just to sow seeds of self-doubt in you. For the sake of peace, sometimes you will have to dim your light and let them shine. Be shrewd and just give them the comfort that they are ahead. This doesn't mean that you are selling yourself short, it is just an effort to not be public enemy number one and it is also a safety measure. Remember that no one is policed like a foreigner, this is a fact that you have to deal with.

Sometimes though, dimming your light doesn't work. No matter how humble a person you try to become, haters are still going to hate. People will always find things to criticize and judge you for. Your humility and modesty can be translated as a pretense, or as you just being fake. So even if you try to accommodate others, they still find ways to fault you. That is why some people do not subscribe to that notion of dimming their light to accommodate others.

You will find yourself in situations where you have to live your life. Trying to empathize with people who do not appreciate your efforts can be exhausting. Yes, you will be called out, you will be called names, people will gossip, but hey, this is the time to do you. Their judgment speaks more about their own character than about yours. Your achievement, no matter how small, proves that you are doing something right. Keep doing what you are doing.

Pace Yourself

Rome wasn't built in one day! As cliché as this saying might sound, it has a profound meaning. A lot of the time we want something so bad that we end up rushing the process of acquiring it. Some even break the law or hurt others, just so they could achieve a certain goal. If results don't show at the time they expected them to, they will surely get disappointed in themselves and feel like failures.

It is only normal that when a person implements change in their life, they wish for the best things to come. This also applies when one relocates to a different country to better their life. The person has hope that they are going to turn their fortune around and live a life of better quality. They hope for a better job, favourable business opportunities, better relationships with others, to have peace of mind and do away with everything that has been holding them back. You are probably also itching to show them back home, that you are now living the life.

All of these are great goals that are also achievable. Having noted that though, it is not a given that relocating will magically take your problems away. It is going to take time, sweat and disappointments here and there before things finally work out for you. If things take time do not despair. Sometimes when things are a bit slow, you can make the mistake of allowing desperation make you work too long and harder. You will look for every opportunity, try to befriend everyone, put yourself out there and so forth. Although you came there for a better life, working without rest is not always a good idea. The unnecessary pressure can invite dire mistakes, or at times danger. Overworking yourself can also bring distractions as well as missed opportunities because you are not working smart.

As much as you wish to reach certain goals, do yourself justice by doing things at your own pace. You might have heard of people who made it big in foreign countries, you can draw inspiration from them, but don't let their experiences put you under pressure. You have no idea how they accomplished their goals. Your goals should be about yourself, and not motivated by the desire to keep up with someone or stay ahead of the pack. Do things according to how you can manage and appreciate any little change that happens. Understand that your pace is the best pace for you. At the end of the day, since you know your own capabilities, the only competition is yourself.

Instead of aiming for being too ambitious, do things according to a schedule of activity and rest. This will help you to make better decisions, produce better results in your work and recharge more quickly. To achieve this, set goals that can be achieved at a reasonable time. Do not rush for things to work out instantly as well as instant gratification. Otherwise, you will crash and burn. Taking things slow doesn't mean that one is being lazy, as much as overworking yourself doesn't make you wise.

Life can be so unpredictable, such that sometimes things don't work out the way you hoped them to. For your own sanity, have space for that. It can take time for you to find a job, for your business to take off, for you to have friends, or for you to accomplish whatever you wanted in your host country. Do not be too hard on yourself, it is what it is and such things happen. Even if you had the best plan, unforeseen circumstances can spoil it all for you. Just try to have more patience, or in some instances implement a different strategy. It's never too late to go back to the drawing board. Avoid worrying too much about what others might say because everyone is wiser when it's not their story.

Celebrate Your Small Wins

As much as you dim your lights to make those around you shine, do not forget to celebrate your wins, no matter how little. Quite often, when people relocate, they hope to strike it big in their host country. This mostly happens to people who are in the creative industry. Feeling that their home country doesn't appreciate the arts that much, they hope that if they move to a more developed country, their talent will be recognized, nurtured and they will be counted amongst international stars.

This has proven true for some of the world's greatest stars. After making that big move, and getting citizenship from developed countries they made it big. Some are multi-award winning actors, supermodels as well as the world's greatest sportsmen and women. Although this is commendable, it must be noted not everyone who relocates has the aim of becoming a renowned star. Do not put yourself under the massive pressure of being all that so that you can shine to your fellow countrymen. As explained in the previous chapters, you might be among those people who moved just to better their lives because the situation at home is difficult.

Even if you don't make it big in your host country, the smallest achievements are also worthy of being celebrated. If you went there for an employment opportunity, the moment you get a job, you should be grateful. In most cases, your first job might not be the one you anticipated, but at the end of the day, it is something. It will pay the bills for now, and also keep you occupied while you are still searching for the job of your dreams. In a world where jobs are not easy to come by, celebrate the fact that you got one. Not everyone gets so lucky, more so foreign nationals. Be proud of yourself, hype yourself, while keeping this as motivation that better things are yet to come.

If you are a student, you will agree that when studying abroad, you need all the motivation you can get. Just like any foreign national, there are going to be times when you feel like an outsider. The language barrier, cultural differences, teaching style and just the general way of life can be a challenge. The fact that you are far from your support network can also be daunting. To keep yourself motivated, set goals that are achievable. It can be improving your marks or working on your social life. Once you achieve something make it a point to celebrate.

You should always reward yourself for achieving anything, no matter how small. Have you made new friends, met a particular deadline, learnt a few words of the local language, nailed cooking a local dish or recently visited a popular place? Then be proud of yourself, you are not merely existing, you are living! You don't have to go all out, just a small treat will do. You can prepare yourself your favourite dish, get some ice cream or chocolate, or take yourself out on a solo date. This motivates you to maintain focus and keep winning. It is also a way to program yourself for bigger achievements and more contentment.

Even if you feel that you haven't achieved something worth celebrating as yet, the fact that you have moved away from your comfort is commendable. You have done something that not a lot of people can ever dream of. The fact that you plucked up the courage to explore the unknown, shows that there is something remarkable about you. Instead of accepting your fate, you decided to do something about it, and that is what winners do.

Don't Forget Where You Come From!

At long last things are going great and life is perfectly fine for you. The hardships are gone, and the fruits of your hard labour are starting to show off. Congratulations on finally finding your breakthrough and experiencing life on the soft side. Sadly, as human beings, sometimes when we strike gold, we forget where we come from. The struggles we have endured to be where we are, get erased from our memories. Even those people who helped us along the road to success become completely invisible. Our mission to reach greatness has been accomplished, and looking back becomes immaterial.

In the event of you making it big in a foreign country, don't make the mistake of forgetting where you come from. Don't make the mistake of looking down on your own people back home, and thinking you are way better than they are. Some people, after moving away from home for just a few years, cannot even speak their mother tongue or stomach the staple food they grew up eating. This normally happens to those who have relocated to more developed countries. They tend to think that they are smarter than their own people, now that they are in countries that are much more advanced.

The fact of the matter is that behaving like that is not a measure of success. Instead, it is pure embarrassment. Just the same as people who move to the city, and suddenly think that those in the village are of a lower class. With such behaviour, you will lose all the respect that people have for you because you reject an important part of yourself. The people who are close to you should remain more or less the same whether you are successful or not. The same applies to the place you come from, it has to have a special place in your heart.

Always remembering where you come from will help you to empathize with those who are now going through the same situation you once tasted. Understanding their struggles will move you to reach out and help where you can. A lot of famous people who have relocated abroad are forever performing generous acts of charity, donations and philanthropy. As much as they are living the life overseas, they still feel for those that are suffering back home. If you have been poor all your life, success might change you into a generous person. This is simply because, you know how it is to have nothing, and how desperate one can get in the quest of making a living.

Our past is also there for us to learn from it. Your past might not be all that rosy, but it is part of what made you who you are today. Sometimes because of what we went through in our past, we might want to put it all behind us. That is fair enough because some people went through misery before their breakthrough. But on the positive side, even the most painful experiences can serve epic lessons. They remind us of where we must never return. Now that you know better, you will try your very best not to become a victim of circumstances again.

Celebrate the fact that you are still here to tell your story. All of this means you are not a quitter, but a fighter. There are those looking at you, and drawing inspiration.

Not forgetting where you come from also shapes where you want to go. A person who looks back can also appreciate the lessons that they have learned and can now make positive choices, both personally and professionally. Your past also reminds you of what got you started, in the first place. Which means it will be easier for you to smash other goals that you have set for yourself. Looking back at your humble beginnings also ignites the fire in you to now reach for the stars. You realize that the sky is the limit and you can be anything that you want to be, regardless of where you are in the world.

Should You Move Back Home?

Not every solution always works out for the best. Sometimes when you try to change your situation for the better, you end up worse off. Sadly, this can happen when you relocate to another country. From getting the right paperwork, employment opportunities, business ventures, to receiving basic needs like health services, you will realize that being a foreigner is not for the fainthearted.

We live in a competitive world, where everyone is trying to put food on the table, and a roof over their head. Times are hard, as both locals and foreigners are looking for opportunities to better their lives. Of course, things will be a lot easier for citizens, as opposed to you. Some jobs and business ventures are only reserved for locals. This is fair enough because charity begins at home. We cannot expect, as an outsider, to have the same privileges as a citizen born and bred there. Understand that life will be a bit harder for you as a foreigner, and you have to work extra hard to get a job or have your own business.

Sometimes trying to get a work or business permit can take time, or in the worst-case scenario, you might not qualify. Hence, it will be impossible for you to get a job legally or open a legitimate registered business. If making a living proves to be hard at the place you have moved to, then you have some tough decisions to make. This might be the time for you to change base. Go to a place where you can get something to sustain yourself. You can opt to move to a different town, district or even another country, where opportunities are available.

When faced with this kind of situation, some people have come to realize that there is no better place than home. Saving themselves all the drama of severe hardships, they moved back home, either temporarily to regroup, or permanently to start a new life with their loved ones around them. You are not a failure by moving back home. It just happens that opportunities cannot accommodate us all. Pat yourself on the back that you at least tried to do something about your situation, it is not your fault that things didn't work out. Do not worry yourself about who will say what about your return. In this life, it is never about how many times you fall, what counts is the number of times you got up and tried again. Who knows, maybe this time around you will find something sustainable at home to make ends meet.

In some instances, foreigners experience xenophobic attacks. Because of high unemployment rates, locals sometimes take out their frustrations on foreign nationals. They burn their shops, property, and continuously protest against having them in their country. In some African countries, foreign African nationals are the most targeted and sadly lives have been lost. This has caused huge animosity between African nationals. If you find yourself a possible target of fierce xenophobic attacks, the best solution might be for you to move. Go to a place where things are calmer. If going back home is the best solution for you, do so without hesitation. You will save your life, and preserve your peace.

Another reason you might consider going back home is because of health issues. If you haven't been well for some time, maybe this is the time for you to go back home. This is very important, more so when you don't have loved ones around. It is better to be around your family who will take care of you better than anyone else. You are also saving them from all the anxiety of constantly worrying about you. You can always come back when you are back in great health.

You don't always have to go back home when things are bad. If you feel you have achieved your goal, then go home. This normally applies to students who have completed their course of study. You can go back home to assist those you left behind with the skills you have acquired. With those skills, you can help create employment opportunities, as well as contribute to the development of your home country.

About the author:

Surviving Unfamiliar Territory is Lebogang Tleane's debut as an author. Lebo, as most people call her was born and raised in her home country Botswana. She moved to South Africa after her marriage in 2015, to join her spouse. She graduated with a degree in Journalism and Media studies from Limkokwing University of Creative Technology.

Lebo has written for a number of publications as a freelancer, and she was the editor of Botswana Youth Magazine for two years. At the moment she is the Managing Editor of Youth Village, a platform that focuses extensively on facilitating better access to developmental information across South Africa with a core focus on the youth.

www.ingramcontent.com/pod-product-compliance
Lightning Source LLC
Chambersburg PA
CBHW021941040426
42448CB00008B/1179